YOUR PET GERBIL

REVISED EDITION

A TRUE BOOK®

by
Elaine Landau

Children's Press®
A Division of Scholastic Inc.

New York Toronto London Auckland Sydney
Mexico City New Delhi Hong Kong
Danbury, Connecticut

Baby gerbils

Content Consultant
Robin Downing, DVM, CVA, DAAPM
Hospital Director, Windsor Veterinary Clinic Windsor, Colorado

Reading Consultant
Cecilia Minden-Cupp, PhD
Former Director, Language and Literacy Program Harvard Graduate School of Education

Author's Dedication
For Klara and Hailey—the world's cutest cousins

The photograph on the cover and the photograph on the title page both show a pet gerbil.

Library of Congress Cataloging-in-Publication Data
Landau, Elaine.
    Your pet gerbil / by Elaine Landau. — Rev. ed.
        p. cm. — (A true book)
    Includes index.
    ISBN-10: 0-531-16768-2 (lib. bdg.)   0-531-15466-1 (pbk.)
    ISBN-13: 978-0-531-16768-7 (lib. bdg.)   978-0-531-15466-3 (pbk.)
    1. Gerbils as pets—Juvenile literature. I. Title. II. Series.
SF459.G4L35 2007
636.935'83—dc22

                                                        2006004419

CHILDREN'S PRESS, and A TRUE BOOK™, and associated logos are trademarks and/or registered trademarks of Scholastic Library Publishing.
SCHOLASTIC and associated logos are trademarks and/or registered trademarks of Scholastic Inc.
1 2 3 4 5 6 7 8 9 10 R 16 15 14 13 12 11 10 09 08 07

Contents

Popular Pets   5

Choosing Your Gerbil   9

A Gerbil Shopping List   17

Caring for Your Gerbil   28

A Great Addition   40

To Find Out More   44

Important Words   46

Index   47

Meet the Author   48

Gerbils are popular pets for children.

Popular Pets

Are you thinking about getting a pet gerbil? Gerbils are popular pets for many reasons.

Gerbils are small. You don't need to have a large house or yard in order to keep them. You also don't need to walk, **groom**, or train a gerbil.

In fact, gerbils produce only a small amount of waste. That means less cleanup work for you!

Some pets can cost a lot of money. You can buy a gerbil for just a few dollars. With proper care, a gerbil can live for three to five years.

The best thing about pet gerbils is the fun you can have with them. Gerbils are intelligent and curious. These eager little explorers will sniff

When you come to its cage, a gerbil will often stand on its hind feet.

out every corner. Don't be surprised if they stand up on their hind feet to greet you. A pet gerbil can bring you hours of joy.

Look carefully before choosing your gerbils.

Choosing Your Gerbil

Gerbils are sold in many pet stores. Go to a clean store that has many gerbils to choose from. A clean store is more likely to care for its animals.

Check out all the gerbils at the store. Be gentle when

Sometimes if you are patient, a gerbil will climb onto your hand.

picking up a gerbil. Rest your hand in the cage for a few minutes. If the gerbil doesn't climb onto your hand, scoop it up carefully with two hands. Never pick up a gerbil by its tail.

Gerbils come in many different colors. They can be solid black, gold, beige, or gray. Gerbils can also have patches of color.

The coats of these gerbils are solid colors.

Whatever color you pick, don't buy just one gerbil. Gerbils like to be with other gerbils. They don't do well alone. A gerbil with a companion tends to be healthier and friendlier than a gerbil that lives alone. It is best to buy gerbils that are between four and eight weeks old.

Are you thinking of buying a male or a female gerbil? Many gerbil owners prefer two females. Sometimes two

Gerbils can keep each other company in the same cage.

male adults will fight. If you buy a male and a female, you could end up with gerbil babies. Then you might have more animals than you can handle!

Taking Home a Healthy Gerbil

A healthy gerbil should have:

* smooth, shiny fur

* clear, bright eyes

* a clean nose

* a solid, plump body

* a curious, active nature

A gerbil with a clean nose and clear eyes

Pass up a gerbil that has:

* a thin coat of fur or any bald spots
* any fluid coming from the eyes
* a runny nose (which could be a sign of illness)
* any cuts or scratches on its body or tail
* no energy

A healthy, energetic gerbil

A healthy gerbil's smooth fur and plump body

15

A gerbil chews on a wood stick, an item on your gerbil shopping list!

A Gerbil Shopping List

Before you bring your little pets home, you will need to buy some supplies. Here is a shopping list of what you will need for your gerbils:

Cage: Gerbils are small, but they need a lot of space.

A gerbil cage should have room for the animal to sleep, eat, play, and explore. You will need a larger cage for a pair of gerbils than you would for a single gerbil.

There are many different kinds of gerbil cages. Pick one that is easy to clean and roomy. An **aquarium**, a glass tank used to keep fish or other small pets, can be a good choice. A simple plastic and wire cage works well, too. Some people choose a plastic cage with tubes for the gerbils to crawl through.

This gerbil cage is made of plastic and wire.

Bedding: Wood shavings make great gerbil bedding. Cover the bottom of the cage with a thick layer of wood shavings. Gerbils love to dig in their bedding.

You can buy wood shavings at any pet store.

Small Pets Bedding

MAKES UP TO 12 HAMSTER GERBIL CAGES

Natural Softwood Flakes

RABBITS · GUINEA PIGS · HAMSTERS · GERBILS · SMALL

A water bottle with a drinking tube keeps a gerbil's bedding and food dry.

Feeding dish and water bottle: Buy a sturdy food dish that won't tip over and a water bottle. Don't use a water bowl because bedding and food will fall into the water.

Nesting box: A **nesting box** is a small container in a gerbil cage. Gerbils hide in a nesting box. Sometimes they take a nap there!

Toys: Gerbils need toys for fun and exercise. You can buy little balls, bells, and ladders made for small animals.

You don't have to spend a lot of money on toys. Cardboard paper towel tubes make wonderful tunnels for your gerbils to explore.

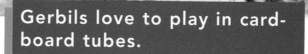

Gerbils love to play in card-board tubes.

Exercise wheel: Gerbils enjoy running and playing on exercise wheels. Be sure to get a wheel with a solid, plastic running surface made for gerbils. Do not get a wire-frame exercise wheel with spokes because a gerbil's long tail can become caught on the wheel.

Wood chew sticks: Your gerbils will need wood sticks to gnaw. These are also sold at pet stores.

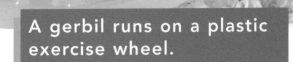

A gerbil runs on a plastic exercise wheel.

Gerbils are **rodents** just like mice, rats, or squirrels. Rodents are animals with two large front teeth for gnawing, called **incisors**. A rodent's incisors are always growing. Gnawing helps trim the incisors.

A gerbil's large front teeth are called incisors.

Gerbil Burrows

A desert gerbil in Algeria

Most wild gerbils live in desert areas. Summers are hot, and winters are cold. Gerbils live in underground tunnels and holes called **burrows**. These burrows are 2 feet (61 centimeters) beneath the ground, where gerbils don't feel the very hot or very cold temperatures.

Gerbil burrows have special areas for nesting and storing food. These large, well-dug tunnels allow gerbils to stay underground for a long time.

Caring for Your Gerbil

Do you have your gerbil and all your supplies? Now you need to find the perfect place for your gerbil cage.

Pick a spot where you and your family will see the gerbils often. Keep the cage away from direct sunlight or

Gerbils are fun to watch and they enjoy company.

cold areas in the house. Put the cage in a safe place, away from other family pets.

29

Gerbils need a clean cage for their health and comfort. You will need to clean the cage once a week. Change all the bedding at this time. You need to replace bedding soiled with gerbil droppings every few days.

You should scrub the water bottle, food dish, and any plastic toys every week, too. The cage should be a place where you would want to live if you were a gerbil!

Your gerbils will appreciate a clean cage.

Food mixes for gerbils often have wheat, oats, barley, corn, pumpkin seeds, and vegetable flakes.

It is important to feed your gerbil a healthy diet. You can feed adult gerbils **food pellets**. Food pellets are small, hard balls of food made for small animals. But don't feed them to young gerbils. They may have trouble breaking the pellets into pieces they can chew.

You can also give your gerbil packaged food mixes. These mixes have just about everything gerbils need.

Feed your gerbils at the same time every day. Don't be surprised if they do not eat all their food at once. Gerbils like to nibble their food throughout the day.

Be sure you are feeding your gerbil fresh food. Check the date stamped on the package and throw it away after that date. If you buy smaller packages of gerbil mix, you are less likely to wind up with stale food.

A gerbil sitting in its food dish nibbles on a seed.

A very active gerbil needs more food than a less active gerbil.

Different gerbils often need different amounts of food. Young, growing gerbils eat more than older gerbils. Male gerbils are larger than females and eat more as well. Active gerbils also eat more.

Pay attention to your gerbils' needs.

Once in a while, you can give your gerbil a treat. But don't expect your pets to make wise food choices.

Dried apples make a tasty treat for your gerbil.

If they can, your gerbils will eat too much of a favorite food, such as sunflower seeds. Then the gerbil may gain too much weight. It is your job to help your pet eat in a healthy way.

If your gerbil should become ill or injured, take it to a **veterinarian** right away. A veterinarian is a doctor who treats animals. Try to find a veterinarian who is used to caring for gerbils.

A veterinarian can help you keep your gerbils healthy.

A Great Addition

It takes work to care for gerbils. But most owners find the pleasures of gerbils outweigh the work of caring for them.

So enjoy your gerbils. Let them out of their cage to exercise often. They will like exploring their surroundings.

A gerbil explores the world outside its cage.

Never leave a gerbil alone when it is out of its cage. Watch your gerbils so they don't get lost or hurt themselves. Gerbils don't know that it is dangerous to chew on an electric cord or eat household plants. Also, never let your gerbil out when a dog or cat is in the room.

A gerbil can be a great addition to your family. These curious, active creatures are sure to make everyone smile.

A gerbil rests in its owner's hand.

To Find Out More

Here are some additional resources to help you learn more about gerbils:

 **Books**

Engfer, LeeAnne. **My Pet Hamster and Gerbils**. Lerner, 1997.

Fox, Sue. **Gerbil Care**. TFH Publications, 2004.

Jeffrey, Laura S. **Hamsters, Gerbils, Guinea Pigs, Rabbits, Ferrets, Mice, and Rats: How to Choose and Care for a Small Mammal**. Enslow, 2004.

Kotter, Engelbert. **My Gerbil and Me**. Barron's, 2002.

Petty, Kate. **Gerbil**. Stargazer Books, 2005.

Silverstein, Alvin, Virginia Silverstein, and Laura Silverstein Nunn. **Pocket Pets**. Twenty-First Century Books, 2000.

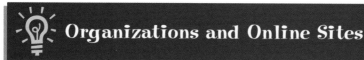

Organizations and Online Sites

American Gerbil Society

http://www.agsgerbils.org/

Check out this site for information on caring for gerbils, various articles about gerbils, and useful links.

American Society for the Prevention of Cruelty to Animals (ASPCA)

424 East 92nd Street
New York, NY 10128
212–876–7700
http://www.aspca.org

This organization's site has extensive information on small pet care, including a brochure on gerbil care that you can download.

National Gerbil Society

http://www.gerbils.co.uk/

This site offers lots of interesting facts about raising gerbils. Click on the link "Gerbil Fun" for paintings of gerbils and wallpaper images of gerbils for your computer.

Pet-parade.com

http://www.pet-parade.com/Gerbils/

Visit this site to get helpful tips from gerbil owners.

Important Words

aquarium a glass tank used to keep fish or other small pets

burrows animal tunnels or holes in the ground

food pellets small, hard balls of food made for small animals

groom to clean an animal

incisors large front teeth

nesting box a small container in a cage that gerbils sleep and hide in

rodents animals with two large front teeth for gnawing

veterinarian a doctor who treats animals

Index

(**Boldface** page numbers indicate illustrations.)

babies, 13
bedding, 20, **20**, 21, **21**, 30
burrows, 27
cages, **7**, **13**, 17–19, **19**, 20, 28–29, 30, **31**
chewing, **16**, 24, 33, 42
cleaning, 30, **31**
colors, 11, **11**
companionship, 12, **13**, **29**
cost, 6
deserts, 27, **27**
exercise, 22, 24, 40
exercise wheels, 24, **25**
exploration, 6–7, 18, 22, 40, **41**
eyes, 14, **14**, 15
feet, 7, **7**
females, 12–13, 36

food, **32**, 33–34, **35**, 36–38, **36**, **37**
food dishes, 21
fur, 14, 15, **15**
handling, 9–10, **43**
incisors, 26, **26**
life span, 6
males, 12–13, 36
nesting boxes, 22
nose, 14, **14**, 15
pets, **4**, 5, 6
rodents, 26
selecting, **8**, 9, 14–15
size, 5
tail, 10, 15, 24
teeth, 26, **26**
toys, **16**, 22, **23**
treats, 37, **37**
veterinarians, 38, **39**
waste, 6
water bottles, 21, **21**
weight, 14, **15**, 38
wood sticks, **16**, 24

Meet the Author

Award-winning author Elaine Landau worked as a newspaper reporter, an editor, and a youth-services librarian before becoming a full-time writer. She has written more than 250 nonfiction books for young people, including True Books on dinosaurs, animals, countries, and food. Ms. Landau has a bachelor's degree in English and journalism from New York University as well as a master's degree in library and information science. She lives with her husband and son in Miami, Florida.